DISCOVER!

ALLERGIES!

I HAVE AN EGG ALLERGY

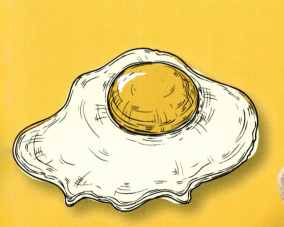

By Kathleen Connors

Please visit our website, www.enslow.com. For a free color catalog of all our high-quality books, call toll free 1-800-398-2504 or fax 1-877-980-4454.

Library of Congress Cataloging-in-Publication Data
Names: Connors, Kathleen, author.
Title: I have an egg allergy / Kathleen Connors.
Description: Buffalo, New York : Enslow Publishing, [2024] | Series: Allergies! | Includes bibliographical references and index. | Audience: Grades K-1
Identifiers: LCCN 2022045119 (print) | LCCN 2022045120 (ebook) | ISBN 9781978533905 (library binding) | ISBN 9781978533899 (paperback) | ISBN 9781978533912 (ebook)
Subjects: LCSH: Food allergy in children–Juvenile literature. | Eggs–Health aspects–Juvenile literature.
Classification: LCC RJ386.5 .C6634 2024 (print) | LCC RJ386.5 (ebook) | DDC 618.92/975–dc23/eng/20220928
LC record available at https://lccn.loc.gov/2022045119
LC ebook record available at https://lccn.loc.gov/2022045120

Portions of this work were originally authored by Kristen Rajczak and published as *I'm Allergic to Eggs*. All new material this edition authored by Kathleen Connors.

Published in 2024 by
Enslow Publishing
2544 Clinton Street
Buffalo, NY 14224

Copyright © 2024 Enslow Publishing

Designer: Claire Wrazin
Editor: Kristen Nelson

Photo credits: Cover (photo) Dragana Gordic/Shutterstock.com; Cover (art, top) Olli_may/Shutterstock.com; Cover (art), pp. 2, 6, 12, 14, 16, 20, 22 Net Vector/Shutterstock.com; Series Art (texture) arigato/Shutterstock.com; p. 5 Photoroyalty/Shutterstock.com; p. 7 Ververidis Vasilis/Shutterstock.com; p. 7 (arrows) Lyudmyla Ishchenko/Shutterstock.com; p. 9 kryshov/Shutterstock.com; p. 11 New Africa/Shutterstock.com; p. 13 Microgen/Shutterstock.com; p. 15 Stephen Barnes/Shutterstock.com; p. 17 Sheila Fitzgerald/Shutterstock.com; p. 19 Andrey_Popov/Shutterstock.com; p. 21 BlueOrange Studio/Shutterstock.com

All rights reserved. No part of this book may be reproduced in any form without permission in writing from the publisher, except by a reviewer.

Printed in the United States of America

Some of the images in this book illustrate individuals who are models. The depictions do not imply actual situations or events.

CPSIA compliance information: Batch #CS24ENS: For further information contact Enslow Publishing, at 1-800-398-2504.

CONTENTS

It's an Allergy! 4

What Happens? 8

Get Tested 12

Don't Eat Eggs! 14

Shots Can Help 18

Maybe Someday! 20

Words to Know 22

For More Information 23

Index 24

Boldface words appear in Words to Know.

¡IT'S AN ALLERGY!

Some foods can make you feel itchy or make your tummy hurt. Eggs are one of the foods many people have an allergy to! An allergy is when the body **responds** to something commonly harmless like it would respond to something harmful.

Egg allergies are one of the most common allergies in kids.

Not feeling well after eating something with egg in it is an allergic **reaction**. The body is fighting the **protein** in the egg! Most people are allergic to egg whites, but the yolk can cause reactions too.

An egg allergy includes eggs from chickens and often eggs from ducks, turkeys, and geese.

7

WHAT HAPPENS?

It's common for an egg allergy to show up first when someone is a baby. The baby might throw up or get a **rash**. Kids and adults with egg allergies might have a runny nose or get a tummy ache after they eat eggs.

It's hard to figure out what is making a baby unwell. Food allergies are often checked first.

An allergic reaction to eggs may include **swelling**. Your heartbeat might speed up. Some people with egg allergies may have a very bad allergic reaction called anaphylaxis (an-uh-fuh-LAK-sis). This means they'll have trouble breathing. They need to see a doctor right away.

If you think you see someone having an allergic reaction, get a grown-up!

GET TESTED

A doctor can let you know for sure it's eggs causing the reaction. They might do a skin test. They'll put a bit of egg **extract** on your skin and **prick** you. If the spot turns red and raised, it's likely an egg allergy.

Skin prick tests are used to test for many different allergies.

DON'T EAT EGGS!

The only way to **avoid** an allergic reaction to eggs is to stop eating them! That also means not eating anything that has eggs in it. Salad dressings, cookies, cake, and pasta may have eggs in them!

Many grocery stores carry foods labeled "egg-free" to help those with egg allergies stay safe.

Checking the **ingredients** in food can help you avoid eggs. Most foods with labels will say if they have eggs in them. There are also other names for eggs you'll need to check for. Make a list and carry it with you!

Some food labels will simply list "eggs" as an ingredient. Others will use different words, such as "albumin."

SHOTS CAN HELP

Rashes, throwing up, or a runny nose caused by an allergic reaction can be treated with **medicines**. Someone with bad allergies needs to carry a shot filled with the medicine epinephrine (eh-puh-NEF-rihn). Someone else can give them this shot if they can't do it themselves.

An epinephrine shot can save the life of a person who has a bad allergic reaction.

19

MAYBE SOMEDAY!

Do you still like the taste of eggs even though you're allergic? Many kids outgrow egg allergies by the time they are 16! So, stay away from eggs right now—but you might not have to forever!

Food allergies are becoming more common in children. You may have friends who can't eat peanuts, milk, or wheat!

WORDS TO KNOW

avoid: To stay away from.

extract: Matter you pull out from something using a machine.

ingredient: One of the things used to make food.

medicine: A drug taken to make a sick person well.

prick: To make a very small hole in something.

protein: A necessary element found in all living things.

rash: A group of red spots on the skin.

reaction: The way your body acts because of certain matter or surroundings.

respond: Something that happens because something else has happened.

swelling: Getting bigger in an uncommon way.

FOR MORE INFORMATION

BOOKS

Orlando, Amanda. *The Easy Allergy-free Cookbook: 85 Recipes Without Gluten, Dairy, Tree Nuts, Peanuts, Eggs, Fish, Shellfish, Soy, Or Wheat.* Emeryville, CA: Rockridge Press, 2022.

Potts, Francesca. *All About Allergies.* Minneapolis, MN: Super Sandcastle, 2018.

WEBSITES

Food Allergies

kidshealth.org/en/kids/food-allergies.html
Read all about why allergies happen here.

Living with Food Allergies

www.kidswithfoodallergies.org/page/living-with-food-allergies.aspx
Learn more about how to stay safe when living with food allergies.

Publisher's note to educators and parents: Our editors have carefully reviewed these websites to ensure that they are suitable for students. Many websites change frequently, however, and we cannot guarantee that a site's future contents will continue to meet our high standards of quality and educational value. Be advised that students should be closely supervised whenever they access the internet.

INDEX

anaphylaxis, 10

egg whites, 6

egg yolk, 6

epinephrine, 18, 19

food labels, 15, 16, 17

itchy, 4

kinds of eggs, 7

medicine, 18

outgrow allergy, 20

rash, 8, 18

runny nose, 8, 18

skin prick test, 12, 13

swelling, 10

throw up, 8, 18

trouble breathing, 10

tummy ache, 4, 8